REAL WORLD ECONOMICS ™

Understanding the Gross Domestic Product and the Gross National Product

CORONA BREZINA

ROSEN
PUBLISHING®
New York

Published in 2012 by The Rosen Publishing Group, Inc.
29 East 21st Street, New York, NY 10010

Library of Congress Cataloging-in-Publication Data

Brezina, Corona.
Understanding the gross domestic product and the gross national product
/ Corona Brezina.
  p. cm.—(Real world economics)
Includes bibliographical references and index.
ISBN 978-1-4488-5569-8 (library binding)
1. Gross domestic product—Juvenile literature. 2. Gross national prod-
uct—Juvenile literature. 3. National income—Juvenile literature. 4.
Economic indicators—Juvenile literature. I. Title.
HC79.I5B725 2012
339.3'1—dc22

                                        2011014677

Manufactured in China

CPSIA Compliance Information: Batch #W12YA: For further information, contact Rosen Publishing, New York,

New York, at 1-800-237-9932.

On the cover: A container ship containing a wealth of goods destined for
export and sale overseas prepares to leave port.

Contents

INTRODUCTION |||

If an economist were asked to sum up a nation's entire economy in a single statistic, he or she would probably cite the gross domestic product (GDP). The GDP is the monetary value of all goods and services produced in a nation during a given time period, usually one year. Basically, it's a tally of everything bought for money during the course of a year. Consumer purchases, from a candy bar to a car, are counted in the GDP. When businesses buy computers, farmers sell their crops, or a corporation exports goods overseas, the transactions all increase the GDP. Government spending, whether for a highway or a new bomber, also contributes to the GDP.

The economist, however, would quickly point out that there is another important related statistic: GDP growth. This figure is a percentage that answers the question, "How fast is the economy growing?" If the annual rate of GDP growth is 3 percent, that means the economy is 3 percent larger than it was the previous year.

Another statistic, gross national product (GNP), is an additional measure of the size of the economy. It uses slightly different criteria than the GDP, and the GDP is more often used for comparison of a nation's economic progress against that of other countries.

The rate of GDP growth changes depending on the health of the economy. During an economic downturn, the economy contracts and GDP declines. The recent recession that lasted from 2007 to 2009 was an exceptionally severe period of economic decline. It was the worst economic downturn since the Great Depression. In fact it was nicknamed the "Great Recession," after that earlier economic catastrophe.

As the United States struggled out of the Great Recession, there was a heightened interest in the quarterly GDP reports. Everyone wanted to hear good news about a hopefully improving economy. A GDP figure that indicated strong economic growth would mean businesses were making more money and

The federal government can provide a jolt to the economy and a boost to the GDP by funding public works projects like highway building and improvements.

that they might start hiring again. Unemployed workers would be more likely to find a job and consumer spending would pick up again, leading to more profit for businesses and even more new hiring.

Government leaders analyze GDP reports when crafting economic policy. The Federal Reserve, which is the central bank of the United States, uses the GDP report to gauge economic activity. Investors look for signs of sustainable economic growth in the GDP report, paying especially close attention to the information it contains on corporate profits. Business leaders also analyze the economy's performance as reflected in the GDP report in order to make decisions on future investment and production.

The GDP is not an all-inclusive measure. It omits some factors that impact a nation's economy, such as unpaid work, the environmental impact of economic activity, and nonmonetary considerations like the value of leisure time. But as a measure of the sheer size of the economy, the GDP provides economists and ordinary citizens alike with a convenient and accurate gauge of economic vitality—or the lack of it.

CHAPTER ONE
MEASURING THE ECONOMY

The gross domestic product is the most important measure of a nation's economy. When economists discuss a nation's economic health and progress, they are more likely to refer to the GDP than any other statistical figure. The gross domestic product and the gross national product both serve as valuable indicators of economic trends.

It might not seem that economic measures have much relevance in the daily lives of ordinary people. Actually, though, every American has a personal stake in a healthy, growing economy. A strong economy supports a high rate of employment. When there are a lot of people in the workforce, they produce more goods and services. They also earn higher wages, meaning that they have more money to spend. As a result, there is an increase in consumer demand, higher retail sales, increased corporate profits, and then even more hiring and higher wages.

An economic downturn produces the opposite effect. If the economy grows at a slower rate, there may not be enough new

Long unemployment lines are a sure sign of economic recession and a shrinking GDP.

jobs created to keep up with population growth. If the economy dips into recession, in which GDP declines, the unemployment rate will rise. Consumer spending falls, as do corporate profits, resulting in even more layoffs. The Great Recession of 2007–2009, for example, saw a drastic increase in the unemployment rate and a dramatic reduction in consumer spending. A prolonged reduction in the GDP during that period provides a precise measure of the depth of the economic downturn.

What Are the GDP and GNP?

A country's GDP is the broadest measure of its economic output. It is defined as the monetary value of all goods and

American autoworkers inspect car engines at a South Korean–owned Hyundai plant in Alabama. The sale of cars made at this plant would contribute to the U.S. GDP, but not its GNP.

services produced in a nation during a given time period, usually one year. The GDP is a very broad and detailed report that adds up the market prices of a huge variety of goods and services.

Goods and services are economic commodities, or things that can be bought for a price. Goods are tangible items, such as food, clothing, appliances, and even roads.

Economists classify goods in many different ways. Durable goods, for example, are items such as refrigerators that are expected to function for a long time. Consumer goods are items purchased by individuals for personal use. Producer goods are purchased by manufacturers. These include categories such as raw materials or tools for use in industrial production.

Services are intangible things that can be purchased. They include everyday activities such as getting a haircut or going out for a movie. But services include a much wider range than most people realize. Health care is an important sector of the service economy. Construction workers provide services. Insurance and investment planning qualify as financial services. Even education is a service. In total, the service sector makes up more than three-quarters of the GDP in the United States.

For the purposes of measuring GDP, goods and services can also be classified as final or intermediate. Final goods and services are intended for the end user—essentially, items and services that are ready for purchase and are to be used or consumed. Intermediate goods and services are used in the production of final goods and services. A car, for example, is a final good. Many of the components of the car, however, are manufactured separately and only later assembled into the car. These components are intermediate goods. GDP does not count the value of intermediate goods. Otherwise, some of the components of the car could be counted twice—during their original production and again as a portion of the value of the finished car. This would cause the GDP to be overstated.

Gross national product is another measure of economic health; it measures the size of a nation's economy. GNP differs from GDP in that it is defined as the monetary value of all goods and services produced by labor and property supplied by the residents of the country. GNP reflects the output of domestically owned enterprises, both within and beyond national borders. GDP reflects the output generated within a nation's borders, whether by domestic or foreign-owned enterprises. For example, GNP would include profits of a General Motors factory located overseas, whereas GDP would not. GDP would include profits of a Toyota plant operating in the United States, whereas GNP would not. The GNP is sometimes referred to as gross national income (GNI).

Calculating GDP and GNP

Since the GDP is the total market value of a nation's goods and services, measuring it is merely an addition equation. GDP is determined by adding up the values of all individual goods and services bought or sold. The figure can be determined using two methods. Economists can add up all the money that has been spent on goods and services—the expenditure approach.

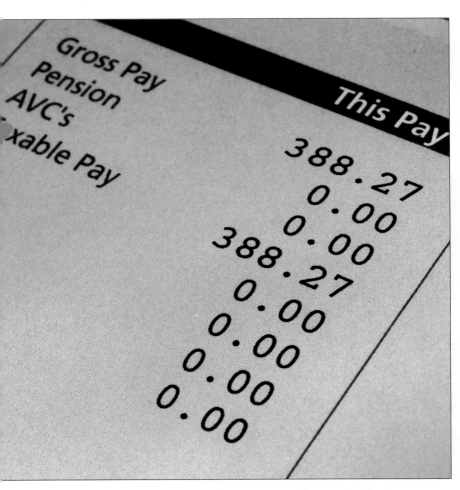

Once taxes have been taken out or paid, an individual's income— what he or she is paid for work—provides him or her with the disposable income necessary to purchase goods and services. These transactions are then factored into the nation's GDP.

Alternately, economists can add up the incomes earned by households—the income approach. Both methods yield the same results. This is because household incomes are equal to expenditures on final goods and services.

The expenditure approach classifies spending within four categories. The biggest category, making up around 70 percent of the total, is consumption expenditures. This is money spent by households on final goods and services. Investment expenditures refer mainly to investments made by businesses, such as on new equipment and manufacturing technology. This category also includes new houses purchased by homeowners. It does not, however, count personal investments, such as buying stocks, bonds, or mutual funds. Government expenditures include government spending on goods and services. The final category is net exports. Americans buy foreign-made products; foreigners also buy American-made products exported to other countries. The value of net exports is determined by subtracting the amount of U.S. expenditures on foreign goods from the amount of foreign expenditures on U.S. goods.

Economists use a mathematical equation to represent the expenditure approach to determining GDP: $GDP = C + I + G + (X - M)$. C is consumption spending, I is investment spending, G is government spending, X is export spending by foreigners, and M is import spending by Americans.

The income approach computes GDP by adding up every different source of household income. The largest component by this method is employee compensation—people's salaries, wages, and other forms of pay. Other sources include rental income, profits from businesses and corporations, and interest

Emphasis on GDP

In 1991, the Bureau of Economic Analysis (BEA), which produces many economic statistics reports, announced that it would begin featuring GDP as the primary measure of U.S. production. Before this, GNP had been the primary measure. The agency cited as a leading reason for the change that GDP covered goods and services "produced by labor and property within the United States" and was therefore a more appropriate measure (even when the labor and property were associated with a foreign-owned company operating in the United States). GNP, by contrast, could include goods and services made overseas (by American-owned companies) as well as American products and services manufactured within the United States.

There were other reasons why the agency supported the change. GDP is more convenient for some statistical purposes. Also, many countries across the world already used GDP as their primary measure of economic production. The BEA's change to GDP made it easier to compare international economic trends using a single standard of calculation.

In general, U.S. GDP and GNP values do not differ much from each other—generally a couple percentage points or less. This is because both U.S. investments abroad and foreign investments in the United States make up a small portion of the entire economy. In other countries, the difference between GDP and GNP is more sizeable. In Great Britain, for example, the GNP is significantly higher than the GDP. This is because many British companies have profitable foreign investments abroad.

payments. In addition to income, some non-income adjust-ments have to be added as well in order to account for the entire GDP. One necessary adjustment is depreciation, which is loss in value of capital goods, such as buildings and equip-ment. The other is indirect business taxes that are not reported by individuals.

GNP is defined as the value of all goods and services produced by the nation's residents. The GNP figure is calculated by making an adjust-ment to GDP. GNP includes income from American assets held abroad—this value must be added to GDP. It excludes income made within American borders by foreign companies—this value must be subtracted from GDP.

Nominal GDP and Real GDP

The expenditure and income calculations for GDP apply the money value of goods and ser-vices. The resulting figure is called the nominal GDP, or sometimes current-dollar GDP. The nominal GDP can be adjusted to calculate a figure called the real GDP. Unlike the nomi-nal GDP, the real GDP takes inflation into account.

In general, overall prices of goods and ser-vices tend to rise gradually over time. This trend is called inflation. Today, $1 does not buy as much as it did fifty or even ten years ago. The rate of inflation is mea-sured in percentages. An annual rate of inflation of 2 percent means that average price levels are 2 percent higher than in the previous year. So something that cost $100 last year now costs $102.

Nominal GDP adds up the values of goods and services based on their prices at the time of production. If the nominal

Paying to see a film at the local movie theater is actually a service transaction. Purchasers never own the services they pay for; they merely enjoy and make use of them for a certain period of time. Buying a DVD of the same film would be a goods exchange, and the purchaser would own the product.

GDP is 4 percent, it indicates economic growth of 4 percent. Ordinary people, however, might not benefit much from a rise in GDP if inflation is also rising. If the rate of inflation is 4 percent, this means that for consumers, the increase in prices cancels out the GDP increase. If the rate of inflation is 2 percent, it still reduces—but doesn't cancel out—the actual effects of economic growth for people when they are buying goods and services. This is because though their incomes may be rising, so, too, are prices, albeit more slowly.

Real GDP is calculated by dividing nominal GDP by a price index figure that adjusts for changes in prices. Since real GDP is based on changes in prices from one year to the next, economists must choose a base year for comparison. The resultant real GDP is smaller than nominal GDP because it considers the effects of inflation.

Per Capita GDP

GDP can be used to determine another useful economic statistic. Per capita GDP, sometimes called "GDP per head," is calculated by dividing a nation's GDP by its population. Since GDP is a nation's total income, per capita GDP is the average income of a resident of that nation.

Per capita GDP adjusts for the different sizes of nations and allows for easy comparison. Two nations may have similar GDP figures, but one nation may have tenfold the population of the other. Despite the equal GDP values, the per capita GDP reveals that the people of the country with the larger population are much poorer. Considering per capita GDP adds a human element to the analysis of the economy. National GDP figures are so huge that it is difficult to gauge proportions.

Putting it in terms of per capita GDP—for example, comparing a nation with a $40,000 per capita GDP against another with a $1,000 per capita GDP—makes the contrast in wealth much more obvious.

Per capita GDP can also be used to track economic growth relative to population. For example, a country may experience a 5 percent growth in GDP over the course of a year. If the population grew by 8 percent, however, the population growth outstrips economic growth. As a result, per capita GDP actually declines slightly.

Per capita GNP can also be calculated by dividing a nation's GNP by its population. Like per capita GDP, it gives an average income per resident and provides a convenient standard of comparison among countries.

CHAPTER TWO

ECONOMIC INDICATORS

If you pay attention to business news, it might seem that every day brings a newly released report of some sort on recent economic trends. The contents of important economic reports may cause stock market values to rise or fall. Analysts discuss whether the data is good or bad news for the economy. The report may or may not correlate with trends of other recent reports. A constant stream of statistics is released on various economic sectors: housing, employment, interest rates, stock market figures, consumer prices, payrolls, unemployment rates, and industrial production. Debate over economic news is especially hot during an economic downturn, when both the general public and finance experts are anxious for any sign of improvement and begin pointing fingers and assigning blame when there is none.

It can be difficult for anyone but an economist to keep track of the endlessly streaming economic figures, especially when they send conflicting messages on economic conditions. But these statistics, when viewed overall, do provide important insights and clues about the general direction in which the economy is heading. Based on the upward or downward changes of some indicators, experts can make forecasts that will be confirmed or challenged by subsequent indicators.

One of the most closely watched economic reports is the gross domestic product report. The figure most anticipated in the report is not the value of the nation's GDP, but the rate of its change—whether the GDP has grown or shrunk and how much. A healthy level of growth is a positive sign for the economy.

GDP and the Business Cycle

Ideally, the GDP maintains a steady, sustainable level of growth. But the economy generally does not stay on a straight, predictable course. It tends to fluctuate through periodic upswings and downswings.

These normal ups and downs of the economy are called the business cycle. It consists of four phases: peak, recession, trough, and expansion. The peak is the point of maximum GDP. From there, the economy enters a recession, a period of downturn in which GDP declines. The bottom of the business cycle is the trough, in which GDP reaches its lowest point. After that, the economy enters a recovery characterized by expansion, a period of GDP growth.

The economy is always going through one of the phases of the business cycle. Historically, long periods of expansion have been interrupted by shorter recessions. A recession is sometimes defined as two or more quarters—six months or more—of declining GDP. The Great Recession began in December of 2007 and ended in June of 2009. Lasting eighteen months, it

Stock prices and the performance of the major stock indexes are considered leading indicators of economic activity. They precede and anticipate major future upward or downward movements of the economy.

was the longest recession since the Great Depression, which occurred during the 1930s.

By contrast, the longest economic expansion in American history took place during the 1990s. A short recession ended in mid-1991. After that point, the economy expanded steadily for almost ten years until the beginning of 2001, when it again dipped into recession.

It would seem that if GDP growth is good for the economy and a nation's citizens, policy makers should try to maximize the GDP growth rate. Actually, though, economists generally agree that a sustained rate of growth around 2.5 percent to 3.5 percent is ideal. At this rate, growth is steady enough that the economy is unlikely to slip into recession and the unemployment rate is likely to remain low.

If the economy grows too quickly, it is likely to be accompanied by a high rate of inflation. Uncontrolled inflation can have a damaging effect on the economy. When it appears that inflation might begin to increase at a dangerous rate, the government can take action to rein it in. GDP growth may be restrained as a side effect of this correction.

OTHER ECONOMIC INDICATORS

Every stage in the business cycle is accompanied by certain economic trends. The GDP reflects the overall state of the economy, but various other measures provide hints regarding the economy's general direction. During a period of economic expansion, for example, businesses hire more workers, so the unemployment rate declines. During a recession, on the other hand, demand for goods and services falls, as do profits. So businesses lay off workers and unemployment levels rise.

When businesses begin to fail throughout several major industries and "Store Closing" signs begin to proliferate, it is a clear sign that the economy is weak and most likely in recession. The drop in sales and production will lead to a shrinking GDP.

Policy makers, economists, and investors use economic indicators to interpret and predict the state of the economy. Economic indicators are data that report activity in different areas of the economy, from corporate profits to sales of

homes. Like the GDP, most economic indicators are released according to a specific schedule. There is often a general prediction of what a particular release will indicate about the economy. If the report's actual findings defy these expectations, it could signal unexpected strength or weakness in the economy, or in one sector of the economy. Often, the significance of a particular indicator can be interpreted in different ways by different economists.

A single indicator is too narrow a measure to gauge the overall health of the economy. Even the most inclusive indicators, such as GDP, are often considered in conjunction with other indicators, such as the unemployment rate. In order to achieve the fullest possible picture of the economy, economists track a variety of indicators and how they shift over time. They can use this information to determine present economic health and predict future economic developments.

Most economic indicators follow cyclical patterns. Economic indicators called leading indicators predict the future state of the economy because they precede the movements of the business cycle. Economists use these indicators to forecast future economic conditions. If there is a disappointing report for one of the leading indicators, such as an increase in new unemployment claims, it could be a troubling sign for the next GDP report. Different leading indicators tend to follow cycles of differing lengths. A peak in housing starts, for example, occurs eight to sixteen months before a peak in GDP. A peak in retail sales, on the other hand, occurs just two or three months before. Other important leading indicators include stock prices, the nation's money supply, interest rates, and consumer expectations.

Coincident indicators accompany GDP results and reflect the current state of the economy and the business cycle. They are useful in confirming economic health or identifying specific concerns in various sectors of the economy. A few coincident indicators include industrial production, personal income, and manufacturing and trade sales.

Lagging economic indicators follow changes to the GDP and are manifested after the major movements of the business cycle. They provide a snapshot of the economy's recent past. One of the most important lagging indicators is the unemployment rate, which generally lags behind GDP by about six months. Therefore, even after a recession ends, the unemployment rate may not begin to fall for half a year. This can be extremely frustrating for workers left jobless after a recession.

THE GDP REPORT

Many of the most important economic indicators are officially released in reports compiled by the Bureau of Economic

MYTHS and FACTS

MYTH The United States has the biggest and fastest-growing economy in the world.

FACT The United States does indisputably have the biggest economy in the world. With a 2010 GDP of more than $14.5 trillion, the U.S. economy is bigger than the next two largest economies combined—China and Japan. The U.S. economy is not, however, the fastest-growing economy in the world. Its 2010 rate of 2.89 percent GDP growth was significantly less than the rate of many developing economies, many of which posted rates between 5 and 10 percent. With these economies growing so quickly, the United States is no longer as dominant in the global economy in terms of sheer size and vitality as it has been in the past.

MYTH If the GDP falls, it's a sign that the economy is in recession.

FACT Economists generally define a recession as two or more quarters (six or more months) of consecutive GDP decline. A long-term drop in GDP is likely an indication that the economy is in recession, but a single quarter of negative growth does not necessarily predict a recession. Also, it takes time to analyze all of the data that determine whether or not the economy is in recession. Economic trends are dated by a government agency called the National Bureau of Economic Research (NBER). The Great Recession ended in June of 2009, but the NBER did not make an official declaration until September of 2010.

MYTH   Per capita GDP measures the standard of living in a country.

FACT   Per capita GDP—the average income per resident of a country—tends to correlate with standard of living, but it is not an official measure of standard of living. The Bureau of Economic Analysis states outright that GDP "is not a measure of well-being (for example, it does not account for rates of poverty, crime, or literacy)." In addition, in nations where much of the wealth is held by a relatively small number of extremely prosperous individuals, per capita GDP does not accurately depict income for the average worker. Where this is the case, median income is likely a better gauge of earnings. At the median level of income, half of all households make more and half make less.

Analysis. An agency within the U.S. Department of Commerce, the BEA collects economic data, analyzes it, and publishes a variety of statistical reports available to the public. The BEA is the agency that determines the official GDP figure for the United States.

The gross domestic product report is released quarterly. Each quarterly report is released in three different versions. One month after the quarter ends, the BEA releases the advance report for the GDP of the previous quarter. A month after that, the second report, a revised version, is released. At this point, the BEA has gathered and analyzed more information. The second report gives a clearer picture of the economy than the advance report and may differ significantly from it in some areas. A month later, the third and final report is released. This report generally does not vary much from the second report. The annual GDP data (GDP data for the entire year) is included in the fourth-quarter GDP report.

Three versions of the fourth-quarter GDP report for 2010 were issued in January, February, and March of 2011. This report also included data on the overall GDP for 2010 and is particularly interesting because it charts the tentative and fragile economic recovery following the two-year-long Great Recession. The report begins with a written summary of the GDP that describes significant contributing factors. The GDP grew at a rate of 3.1 percent in the fourth quarter, revised from an advance estimate of 3.2 percent and a second estimate of

When more and more people are losing their jobs, consumer confidence plummets and spending slows. Stores are forced to sell their goods at a steep discount to attract cautious shoppers. The lack of spending and the reduced profits are both reflected in a smaller GDP.

2.8 percent. The report goes on to summarize trends in growth and downturns. Personal consumption and export revenue, for example, increased in the fourth quarter of 2010. Government spending generally decreased. There was a decline in imports, which contributed to growth because import spending is subtracted in calculating GDP. Price levels increased by 2.1 percent. The report lists the current-dollar GDP, or nominal GDP, of the fourth quarter, which was 3.5 percent. The total value of GDP was $14,861 billion. The report also summarizes the GDP figures for the entire year of 2010. The rate of GDP growth was 2.89 percent, and prices increased 1.2 percent.

Following this summary are a series of tables that examine the component figures of GDP and compare them to previous years. This includes the four main categories—consumption, investment, exports, and government—and breaks these down further into subcategories. Another table lists GDP values and figures for various accounts going back fifteen years. In 2009, the rate of GDP growth was −2.6 percent. This means that due to the recession, GDP actually declined. The rate for 2008 was 0.0 percent. All of the previous years reported positive growth, ranging from 1.1 percent in 2001 to 4.8 percent in 1999.

The BEA also calculates GNP value and includes it in some of the tables. The GNP for the fourth quarter of 2010 was 2.8 percent. The GNP for the entire year of 2010 was 3.1 percent.

CHAPTER THREE

GDP AND GNP IN THE GLOBAL ECONOMY

||||||||||||||||||||||||||||||||||

Due to factors such as technological advances, reduction of trade barriers, and expansion of international financial markets, the world's economies are more interconnected than ever before. And the weakness of one can affect the health of them all. An internal crisis that affects the financial health of one country can send shockwaves around the world. For example, the Great Recession was not confined to the United States—nations around the world experienced downturns of varying degrees in the growth of their gross domestic product in 2008. As the U.S. economy staged a recovery beginning in 2010, economies across the globe also began to rebound.

Most governments of the world maintain a national accounting system that compiles various measures of economic activity. There is even a set of international guidelines,

In the wake of the global recession of 2007–2009 that began in the United States, Ireland got swept up in its own debt and housing market crisis. These protestors in Dublin vent their anger over the Irish government's harsh austerity measures put in place to curb spending and reduce national debt.

the System of National Accounts, that provides guidelines on measuring GDP and other key statistics.

COMPARING GDP OF DIFFERENT NATIONS

When computing GDP, nations use their local currency. In order to compare it to the GDPs of other countries, it must first be converted to a common currency. For example, Great Britain's GDP in 2009 was £1,393 billion—the British unit of currency is the pound sterling (£). In dollars, the figure equaled $2,178 billion, according to the International Monetary Fund (IMF).

Converting values of currency, however, may result in an incomplete understanding of the true worth of money in a foreign nation's economy. The same goods and services do not cost the same amount in every country. In addition to asking how much local currency equals in U.S. dollars, one should ask how much the value of a dollar will buy in that country.

This concept is illustrated by the fanciful "Big Mac Index," invented by the British magazine the *Economist*. More than a hundred nations of the world sell the McDonald's hamburger the Big Mac, but the price varies greatly from one country to another. In 2010, the Big Mac sold for $3.73 in the United States. In China, a Big Mac cost $1.95 U.S. after currency conversion. In Norway, it was $7.20. This means that a single dollar will buy almost twice as many Big Macs in China as in the United States, but only about half as many in Norway.

The Big Mac Index shows that the dollar has a different purchasing power in different countries. An alternate kind of exchange rate called Purchasing Power Parity (PPP) takes this discrepancy into account when considering GDP. It tallies the

RATES PER £1.00	WE SELL	WE BUY
U.S.A.	1.52	1.6
BELGIUM	47.87	51.4
CANADA	2.035	2.2
DENMARK	8.75	9.6
FRANCE	7.80	8.4
GERMANY	2.30	2.5
IRELAND	0.96	1.0
ITALY	2350	254
JAPAN	165	18
NETHERLANDS	2.60	2.8

In order to accurately compare the GDP of one or more nations, the various national currencies must be converted to a single currency that is chosen as the standard. On this currency exchange board, the national currencies are converted to the British pound. Then, the different purchasing power of that currency in each country must be accounted for because a British pound would buy far less in Norway than it would in China or Mexico.

| SWITZERLAND | 1.86 | 2.0 |
| MIN'CHARGE £ | 3.00 | 3.0 |

prices of a representative basket of goods and services across national borders using a single currency—say, the dollar—converted into local currency. When the dollar will buy greater or lesser amounts of goods and services than it would in the United States, the GDP is adjusted upward or downward in proportion.

A comparison of a nation's fixed currency GDP with its PPP-adjusted GDP sometimes offers two significantly different figures. In 2009, China's GDP was $4,985 billion. Adjusted for PPP, it was $9,047 billion. By contrast, Norway—nation of the expensive Big Mac—had a GDP of $379 billion. Norway's PPP-adjusted GDP was $252 billion. As for the United States' neighbors, Canada's GDP of $1,336 billion differed little from its PPP-adjusted GDP of $1,278 billion. Mexico, however, reported a GDP of $875 billion and a much higher PPP-adjusted GDP of $1,464 billion. In Canada, a dollar will buy about the same amount of goods and services as in the United States, but in Mexico, it will buy more than one-and-a-half times the amount.

PPP-adjusted GDP figures are useful in comparing the strengths of different economies. Some PPP adjustments are inexact, however, especially for developing nations. GDP derived from official exchange rates is more appropriate for calculating official economic statistics. GNP can also be adjusted for PPP.

GLOBAL GDP

The world GDP—the sum of the GDP of every country—is currently almost $60,000 billion. The United States, with a GDP of nearly $15,000 billion at the end of the first decade of the twenty-first century, has the largest economy in the world.

A factory in Shanghai, China, produces steel sheets for use in automobiles. This company produces half of all the steel sheets needed by the Chinese auto industry. An explosion in Chinese production of goods, especially for export, has catapulted the nation's economy into the number-two spot worldwide, behind only the United States.

The combined GDPs of the members of the European Union, however, slightly exceed the GDP of the United States.

In 2010, China became the world's second largest economy, with a GDP of $5,745 billion. Japan, with a GDP of over

$5,000 billion, is the world's third largest economy. After the devastation of World War II, Japan's economy rebounded, and its industrial capabilities quickly made it a global economic power in the postwar decades. Economic growth stagnated during the 1990s, however. Since 1991, Japan's annual GDP growth rate has failed to top 3 percent.

Germany is currently the world's fourth largest economy, with a GDP of over $3,000 billion. With a strong industrial base, Germany is Europe's economic powerhouse and leading exporter. France, Great Britain, and Italy currrently have the fifth, sixth, and seventh largest economies. All three of these European nations saw moderate rates of growth during the first decade of the twenty-first century, with annual rates infrequently exceeding 3 percent.

Brazil has the world's eighth largest economy, with a GDP of over $1.500 billion. Like China, Brazil is a developing nation that has seen impressive economic growth in recent years. In discussing nations with rapidly developing economies, economists sometimes use the acronym BRIC, representing Brazil,

China's Economic Boom

The People's Republic of China experienced meteoric economic growth during the first decade of the twenty-first century. In 2000, China was the world's sixth largest economy, with a GDP of $1,252 billion. By 2010, it had moved up to become the world's second biggest economy. Its annual GDP growth over the decade ranged from 8.3 percent in 2001 to 14.2 percent in 2007. In 2000, China's per capita GDP was under $1,000. By 2009, it had nearly quadrupled to $3,734, a figure still far below the international average, however.

China's growth resulted primarily from profitable foreign trade. Every year, the United States runs a trade deficit with China. This means that the United States buys far more Chinese goods than China buys from the United States. Since 2005, the trade imbalance has exceeded $200 billion every year, according to the U.S. Census Bureau.

Despite its continuing favorable prospects, China's economy faces challenges in the future. The economy must maintain a high level of growth in order to create enough jobs for new entrants into the workforce. If the economy flags, the government could face social unrest from a population still adjusting to economic development. The nation must also address environmental issues, such as air pollution and soil erosion, that affect crops and worker health. A high rate of inflation, always a distinct danger in a rapidly expanding economy, could also cause highly disruptive economic problems.

Russia, India, and China. These are four countries that are leading the global economy in economic expansion. As these nations become wealthier, they create new global markets for goods and services and consume more of the world's natural resources. South Korea has also seen impressive economic growth in recent years.

Listing the nations of the world by PPP-adjusted GDP, rather than by official exchange rates, changes the ranking slightly. The United States, China, and Japan still top the list, but China's PPP-adjusted GDP currently exceeds $9,000 billion, almost double its official exchange rate GDP. India edges out Germany for fourth place, and Russia moves up to sixth place, ahead of Great Britain.

The total value of a nation's GDP gives an idea of its position on the global economic stage, but it does not indicate much about personal wealth or standards of living within the country. A large GDP does not absolutely guarantee that a nation's residents are wealthy or even well-off on average. Similarly, the nations with the smallest GDPs do not necessarily have the world's poorest residents. The small GDP could merely reflect an extremely small population.

STANDARDS OF LIVING

Unlike regular GDP, per capita GDP does provide a measure of how a nation's income is distributed among its residents. Per capita GDP is a useful yardstick for gauging the standard of living within a country. The populations of nations that report higher per capita GDPs generally have an overall higher standard of living. Per capita GDP is not, however, an official measure of standard of living.

As a whole, the average North American enjoys a high standard of living, with access to clean water, reliable and high-tech infrastructure, good medical care, high life expectancy, low infant mortality, decent incomes and housing, and good educational and employment opportunities. These Chicago residents are enjoying a sunny afternoon by Lake Michigan.

What exactly is meant by standard of living? Basically, it is the financial well-being of a population, as determined by a number of measurable factors. The residents of a nation with a high standard of living usually have high incomes and low rates of poverty.

They have access to employment, affordable health care, decent housing, and quality education. They live in a nation that usually offers reliable infrastructure, a stable political system, freedom of religion and expression, and quality environmental conditions. Standard of living is also linked with the health of a population. Countries with a high standard of living have higher life expectancies, lower rates of infant mortality, and lower rates of certain diseases and health conditions.

In recent years, the world average per capita GDP has been over $8,500. In a list of nations with the highest per capita GDP, the United States currently occupies ninth place, with a per capita GDP of over $45,000. Populous nations with higher per capita GDPs include Norway, Switzerland, Denmark, and the Netherlands. Most of the countries in western Europe appear in the top twenty-five, as do Australia, New Zealand, and Japan.

Many of the developing countries with high national GDPs are not ranked near the top when per capita GDP is considered. China, with a current per capita GDP of over $3,500, is ranked 95th; India, at over $1,000 is ranked 132nd. This is because both nations have massive populations, with more than a billion people each. Russia and Brazil, each with per capita GDPs of over $8,000, occupy the 52nd and 56th spots, respectively. The relatively low ranking of these emerging economies indicates that much of the population lacks some of the resources and opportunities more widely available in the developed world.

The countries at the bottom of the list—about forty in total—report per capita GDPs of less than $1,100. This means that, on average, residents must live on less than $3 a day. Most of these countries are in Africa, with a few in Asia. Many of these nations have experienced war or social unrest in the past decade.

Per capita GDP can also be PPP-adjusted. Since these figures take into consideration the buying power of people's money, emerging economies tend to rank higher on a list of PPP-adjusted per capita GDPs. In recent years, China had a PPP-adjusted per capita GDP of $6,778; India, $3,015; Brazil, $10,499; and Russia, $14,913.

There are problems in equating per capita GDP too closely with standard of living. Economists do not take standard-of-living factors into account in reporting GDP—it is intended as a purely economic measure. Also, since per capita GDP is calculated by dividing GDP by population, it results in a perfectly even distribution of income. In reality, GDP is never perfectly distributed. In some nations, the richest 1 percent of the population possesses the majority of a nation's wealth. The amount of national income held by the majority of the population is therefore often far smaller than indicated by per capita GDP figures.

CHAPTER FOUR

GDP LIMITATIONS

Gross domestic product is a precise and comprehensive economic indicator. Some critics claim, however, that GDP is overemphasized as a gauge for a nation's economic health.

One argument focuses on what goes into GDP and how it is determined. Some types of transactions do not fit into any of the income or expenditure categories used in calculating GDP. Therefore, these are not accounted for, even though they may contribute to economic growth. Also, GDP does not examine the nature of the economic activities that do lead to economic growth. Some economic activities increase annual GDP growth and foster long-term economic growth. Other contributors to short-term GDP growth may actually harm long-term economic prospects.

Another argument makes the case that policy makers and economists should consult some alternative index to GDP in assessing a nation's prosperity. In general, economists do not claim that GDP has much political significance beyond

These volunteers are preparing for a day of work at a food bank run by the Community Kitchen of West Harlem in New York City. Volunteer work—and whatever goods and services are exchanged during it—are not counted in the nation's GDP.

its purpose of measuring a nation's economic activity, which makes it a valuable tool in crafting economic policy. Some experts believe, however, that if a nation's overall progress is to be expressed in a single statistic, that statistic should also take

into account factors such as standard of living and even quality of life.

MISSING FROM GDP

GDP measures values of goods and services that are produced and then sold for money. It does not include nonmarket transactions or economic activities that are not reported to the government.

Nonmarket transactions include unpaid labor of various kinds, such as volunteer work or housework. If you take a cab, eat out for lunch or dinner, hire a cleaning service, or have your nails done, each of these transactions contributes toward the national GDP. If you drive your own car, make your own lunch or dinner, clean your own house, and manicure your own nails, however, none of these activities are counted in the GDP. Nonmarket transactions are excluded from GDP because they would be very difficult to assess in value. It would also be challenging to decide which types of transactions to include and which to reject.

The value of nonmarket interactions should not be dismissed. The jobs Web site Salary.com determines an annual "stay-at-home mom salary" based on surveys. Recently, the site

No matter how much money sidewalk vendors rake in when they sell consumer goods—whether authentic or knock-off—without authorization, not a dime of it will be counted toward the GDP. The sales are unrecorded, and no taxes are paid on the purchase or the income.

calculated that if stay-at-home parents were paid for the value of their work, they would earn $117,856 annually.

The prevalence of nonmarket transactions is even higher in less developed nations. In these countries, more people produce their own goods for household use and help out neighbors for free. People are also more likely to barter for goods and services than in industrialized nations.

GDP does not include transactions in the underground, or shadow, economy, made up of legal economic activities that go unreported to the government, as well as illegal activities. The term "shadow economy" might immediately bring to mind the black market, but unreported legal business activities actually make up a greater value than illegal activities. Of the illegal activities, tax evasion is one of the most common and a major aspect of the underground economy (as when workers are paid in cash to avoid payroll and income taxes). Illegal business activities can bring in huge profits; the global drug trade alone generates hundreds of billions of dollars every year. Other profitable illegal activities include bribery, prostitution, gambling, fraud, and sales of stolen goods.

Estimating the value of the underground economy is very difficult. Most official reports tend to focus on statistics for unreported legal activities. In general, nations with higher taxes and complex tax laws tend to have higher rates of activity in the underground economy. The United States has one of the smallest shadow economies of the world, with a rate of about 8.6 percent of official GDP (as estimated by economist Friedrich Schneider). Most

Cleanup and rebuilding efforts following natural disasters like the 2011 tsunami in northern Japan can stimulate the economy and boost the GDP. But the costs to survivors—both material and emotional—are enormous and can never be adequately relieved.

high-income European countries, as well as Japan, China, New Zealand, and Australia, have rates between 10 and 25 percent. Developing countries tend to have rates twice as high. Russia, which is notorious for its black market and organized

crime, has a level of 43.8 percent. By region, sub-Saharan Africa has the highest level of transactions occurring in the underground market.

Another criticism of GDP is that it does not account for the cost of negative externalities, or spillover effects, of economic growth. Industrial production often emits air, soil, and water pollution. Corporations make profits off of their products, which contributes to GDP. The residents of the surrounding area, however, may be subjected to the costs—economic, health, and otherwise—of the pollution, and these costs are not reflected in GDP.

Similarly, the GDP computations do not consider the nature of the economic activities that may spur growth. Natural disasters, for example, require extensive cleanup and rebuilding efforts. Hurricane Katrina in 2005 was one of the greatest natural disasters in recent American history. The reconstruction work that followed boosted GDP because of the amount of economic activity generated. The *Exxon Valdez* oil spill of 1989 also required high levels of spending that likewise increased GDP. The earthquake and

Green GDP

If a nation were to clear-cut all of its forests for a profit, it would contribute to positive GDP growth. Similarly, goods and services obtained from mining, oil production, and other development of nonrenewable natural resources increase the GDP. Even outright environmental damage done in the name of development and profits can grow the economy. If the Environmental Protection Agency (EPA) orders a polluting company to clean up a hazardous site, the company may contest it in court. GDP is increased by the legal wranglings—paid both by the company and the government on behalf of the EPA for lawyer services and court administrative costs. If upheld, the GDP is even increased by the eventual cleanup. If people were sickened by the polluted site, their health care costs would also contribute to economic growth. Clearly, a growing GDP doesn't necessarily reflect an entirely rosy picture for the nation as a whole. The economy may be growing, but at a cost that is ruinous to the health and well-being of the environment, wildlife, and human communities.

For this reason, most proposed alternate indexes to the GDP include an environmental component. The value of environmental damage could be subtracted from the index, much as the value of depreciation is subtracted from GDP. The difficulty comes with assigning monetary values to environmental factors. Assessing the value of an oil field is fairly straightforward. Evaluating health care costs related to air pollution from a factory is far more difficult. Putting a price tag on an endangered species gone extinct or on damages from climate change would involve an intense political debate.

In 2005, China attempted to establish a measure of "green GDP." The report showed that the costs of pollution decreased GDP by 3 percent—a figure widely believed to be an underestimate. For the government, a 3 percent reduction in growth was too great to admit to or acknowledge. In order to boost its GDP figures, promote confidence in its economy, and avoid bad press, China has since ceased publishing its green GDP figure.

resulting tsunami that devastated northern Japan in 2011 was expected to cost billions of dollars. Yet the rebuilding and spending projects were likely to provide a significant boost to an economy that had been stagnant for more than twenty years. Yet Japan's growing post-disaster GDP would not fully or truly reflect the utter devastation wreaked on millions of lives.

GDP also suffers from tunnel vision in that it does not consider the sustainability or long-term impact of activities that stimulate economic growth. An economic sector that relies on a finite natural resource, for example, may increase annual GDP, but its long-term prospects are limited (such as oil and other fossil fuel–dependent industries). Health care spending is a significant sector of the economy, but it does not build a nation's wealth.

More National Accounting

GDP and GNP reports are both types of national accounts— data sets on the income and production of goods and services within an economy. The GDP is a very broad indicator, and it can be honed down to give a better idea of how much the average earner actually takes home.

For example, net domestic product (NDP) can be calculated by subtracting depreciation from GDP. Depreciation is the loss of income due to factors such as wear and tear on buildings and equipment. National income (NI) is calculated by subtracting certain business taxes from NDP. Personal income (PI) is an adjustment of NI that determines the income that households actually receive. It deducts some financial categories, such as corporate profits, and adds others, such as income from interest. Finally, disposable personal income (DI) is calculated by subtracting personal taxes. This is the amount of income that households actually have available for meeting expenses once taxes are paid.

The GDP is the best-known national account released by the Bureau of Economic Analysis, but the agency also publishes a number of related accounts. Its report on personal income and outlays tracks what people earn, how much they save, and how much they spend on goods and services. The corporate profit report focuses on corporate earnings. The fixed assets report tracks capital stocks and durable goods, and it allows for an estimate of depreciation. Another account tracks research and development investment. The BEA also reports

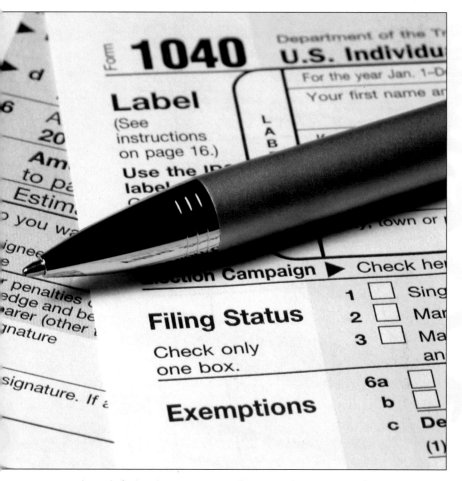

Though federal income taxes bite into the amount of money one has to spend on goods and services, tax dollars are spent by the government on goods and services that benefit all citizens. This government spending boosts GDP, stimulates the economy, and supports higher levels of employment and production in both the public and private sectors.

on industry accounts, international accounts, and regional accounts, which include GDP measures for each state in the United States.

Beyond GDP and GNP

Many economists and world leaders have expressed concern over the reliance of governments on GDP measures in formulating their nations' economic policies. This is not necessarily a criticism of GDP itself. The critics' primary argument is that, along with economic activity, policy makers should weigh environmental sustainability and social issues.

Some experts have proposed that rather than developing a new measure outright, policy makers should consult a "dashboard" that includes complementary indicators along with GDP. In a 2007 European Union conference, the European Commission proposed setting up two new indexes. The environmental index would measure progress in environmental protection, tracking trends such as climate change, biodiversity, water pollution, and use of resources. A second index would measure quality of life.

Considering social as well as economic aspects in measuring a nation's well-being is not a new idea. One of the best-known alternate systems of economic measuring is the human development index (HDI), established in 1990. HDI ranks countries in order of how well they provide their citizens with the means of leading full, productive lives. It is administered by the United Nations Development Programme, which issues an annual Human Development Report.

Citizens' access to higher education, especially high-quality and affordable higher education, is an important measure of a nation's quality of life and its likely competitiveness in the global economy.

HDI uses three criteria in determining rankings: life expectancy at birth, level of education achieved, and PPP-adjusted gross national income (GNI), which is the same as GNP. These categories represent the health, education, and living standards of a country's residents. HDI uses GNP, not GDP, for its economic component. GDP measures the value of goods and services produced within a nation's borders, whereas GNP measures the income of a country's residents. Therefore, GNP is more appropriate for HDI's analyses.

HDI sorts nations as very high, high, medium, or low human development. Norway currently leads the list, followed by Australia, New Zealand, and the United States. Most European nations, as well as Japan, are included in the very high category. Most South American and Asian nations fall into the high to medium categories; China is now near the top of the medium list. Many of Africa's nations are categorized as low.

There have been other attempts to incorporate standard of living into measures of economic well-being, but none have seen widespread use. The genuine progress indicator (GPI) takes positive and negative aspects of economic activities into account. The gross national happiness, used by the Asian nation of Bhutan, intentionally rejects the emphasis of GDP on production and consumption in favor of measuring individual and collective happiness as a public good.

CHAPTER FIVE

GDP AND ECONOMIC DOWNTURNS

Today, we take gross domestic product for granted. When GDP figures and reports on other economic indicators are released, they briefly receive attention in the national news before being superseded by the next set of economic statistics. Any researcher or student can find archived GDP reports on the Internet. A wealth of other economic statistics on nations across the world is easily available as well.

If the U.S. government suddenly announced that it was going to stop issuing economic reports, it might not seem like a big deal to the average citizen. But this would be cataclysmic for policy makers and businesspeople. The president and Congress, in setting the nation's budget, would not know if the economy was growing or contracting. The Federal Reserve would not be able to counteract a recessionary cycle or inflationary pressures. The stock market would be unable to judge the prosperity of the nation's corporations. Business leaders would not know the level of consumer demand for goods and

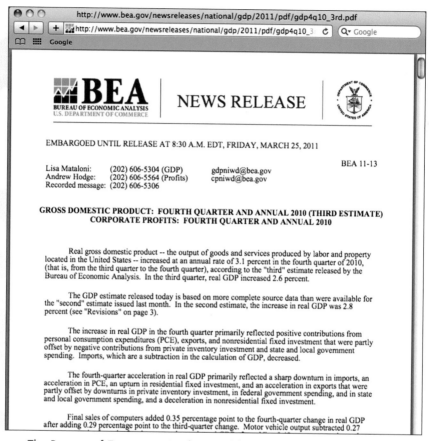

http://www.bea.gov/newsreleases/national/gdp/2011/pdf/gdp4q10_3rd.pdf

http://www.bea.gov/newsreleases/national/gdp/2011/pdf/gdp4q10_3

Google

BEA NEWS RELEASE

BUREAU OF ECONOMIC ANALYSIS
U.S. DEPARTMENT OF COMMERCE

EMBARGOED UNTIL RELEASE AT 8:30 A.M. EDT, FRIDAY, MARCH 25, 2011

BEA 11-13

Lisa Mataloni: (202) 606-5304 (GDP)   gdpniwd@bea.gov
Andrew Hodge: (202) 606-5564 (Profits)   cpniwd@bea.gov
Recorded message: (202) 606-5306

GROSS DOMESTIC PRODUCT: FOURTH QUARTER AND ANNUAL 2010 (THIRD ESTIMATE)
CORPORATE PROFITS: FOURTH QUARTER AND ANNUAL 2010

Real gross domestic product -- the output of goods and services produced by labor and property located in the United States -- increased at an annual rate of 3.1 percent in the fourth quarter of 2010, (that is, from the third quarter to the fourth quarter), according to the "third" estimate released by the Bureau of Economic Analysis. In the third quarter, real GDP increased 2.6 percent.

The GDP estimate released today is based on more complete source data than were available for the "second" estimate issued last month. In the second estimate, the increase in real GDP was 2.8 percent (see "Revisions" on page 3).

The increase in real GDP in the fourth quarter primarily reflected positive contributions from personal consumption expenditures (PCE), exports, and nonresidential fixed investment that were partly offset by negative contributions from private inventory investment and state and local government spending. Imports, which are a subtraction in the calculation of GDP, decreased.

The fourth-quarter acceleration in real GDP primarily reflected a sharp downturn in imports, an acceleration in PCE, an upturn in residential fixed investment, and an acceleration in exports that were partly offset by downturns in private inventory investment, in federal government spending, and in state and local government spending, and a deceleration in nonresidential fixed investment.

Final sales of computers added 0.35 percentage point to the fourth-quarter change in real GDP after adding 0.29 percentage point to the third-quarter change. Motor vehicle output subtracted 0.27

The Bureau of Economic Analysis publishes quarterly reports on the nation's GDP. In each quarter, an initial report is released, followed by two revised reports. The fourth-quarter report also includes a year-end GDP estimate.

services. During ordinary times, this would cause chaos. If the nation were in the midst of an economic downturn on the level of the Great Recession, it would be catastrophic.

Believe it or not, this is nearly how the state of economic affairs stood before the Great Depression. National accounts are a relatively new conception. Before the 1930s, there was no systematic measurement of national income. As the Great

Depression set in, the government could only broadly estimate the scale of the economic consequences.

THE DEVELOPMENT OF NATIONAL ACCOUNTING

In 1932, the United States was in the midst of the Great Depression, which had begun in 1929. In attempting to craft policy to combat the economic crisis, the government was hampered by a lack of information on national income and output. President Herbert Hoover had sent out six Department of

Simon Kuznets won a Nobel Prize in economics, in part for his groundbreaking work on developing the GNP and other essential benchmarks and measures of national income. His efforts helped government economists grasp the scope of the crisis during the Great Depression and finally take effective steps to combat it.

Commerce employees to investigate the true state of the economy. They returned with stories and observations, but very little measurable data. Frustrated, members of Congress passed a resolution requiring the Department of Commerce to develop a broad set of data on economic activity.

The task fell to economist Simon Kuznets of the National Bureau of Economic Research, working with a small committee and a tiny budget. Nonetheless, Kuznets succeeded in compiling a statement of national income that laid the groundwork for all subsequent developments in the field. He presented his findings in a 1934 report, *National Income, 1929–32*. For the first time, there was a methodical and comprehensive summary of economic progress that included a national income, broken down by each sector of the economy.

In the report, Kuznets also examined how national income changed over time. His tables of data and statistics clearly showed the economy deteriorating between 1929 and 1932. Eventually, Kuznets compiled data on the American economy dating back to 1869. He also helped develop the formal GNP system, which was introduced in 1942, in part to help facilitate the war production effort.

THE GREAT DEPRESSION BY THE NUMBERS

Examination of GDP and other economic indicators reveals the extent of the worst economic downturn in American history.

During the so-called Roaring Twenties, many Americans went deep into debt buying new consumer goods. They were therefore not financially prepared for an economic downturn. In late 1929, the stock market crashed. At its peak, the stock

Bank runs—when depositors reacted to rumors about a bank's imminent failure by crowding in and clamoring for their savings— were a common phenomenon during the Great Depression. As a direct result of these panics, bank deposits are now insured up to $250,000.

market index stood at 386.10. By mid-1930, it declined to its lowest point of 41.22.

The shock waves from the crash impacted the entire economy. Consumers cut their spending, and, as a result, business profits plummeted. In response, businesses cut production and laid off workers. The unemployment rate rose as high as 25 percent at the height of the Depression. People couldn't pay off their debts, and this impacted the banking system. Many banks failed, and the surviving banks were wary about issuing new loans. Deflation—a general decline in prices—further crippled the economy.

In his *National Income, 1929–32*, Kuznets reported that over that time period, national income declined by 50 percent. Every sector of the economy except for government spending had declined, with manufacturing income falling by 70 percent. GDP figures from BEA archives show that the rate of growth was negative for four years straight through 1933, with a staggering 13.1 percent decline in growth for 1932. Altogether, GDP declined nearly 30 percent throughout the Great Depression.

The government attempted to counteract the Great Depression with a package of fiscal policy measures called the New Deal, as well as monetary policy. As a result, GDP grew by 10.9 percent in 1934, and it maintained relatively high rates of growth for several years afterward.

DEALING WITH ECONOMIC DOWNTURNS

GDP figures provide a valuable interpretive and policy-making tool for dealing with economic downturns. By analyzing GDP and other indicators, policy makers can anticipate a slowdown

Female workers assemble the tail fuselage section of a B-17 "Flying Fortress" bomber in Long Beach, California, in 1942. The spike in industrial output and military spending in advance of American entry into WWII and during the war years finally helped propel the United States out of the Great Depression.

and identify weak areas in the economy. Before World War II, recessions generally lasted for nearly two years, partly because economic data was lacking that would allow for an effective policy response. For the second half of the twentieth century, recessions were shorter—less than a year on average—and they occurred less frequently. Economists give some credit for this shift to data provided by GDP that now allow for timely and appropriate intervention measures.

The economy experienced ten periods of recession between the end of World War II and the Great Recession of 2007–2009. Mobilization for the war had finally allowed the U.S. economy to rebound from the devastation of the Great Depression. GDP soared during the war years, increasing by 17.1 percent in 1941, 18.5 percent in 1942, and 16.4 percent in 1943. Some economists feared that a transition back to peacetime would bring high unemployment, with soldiers returning from overseas looking for work. They also feared inflation because wartime price controls had been removed. A mild recession did indeed occur during 1948 and 1949, but real GDP dropped by only 2 percent. Minor recessions also occurred during 1953–54, 1957–58, 1960–61, and 1969–70.

Throughout the years, the BEA has continued making improvements to the statistics, concepts, and overall framework of national accounting. In the late 1960s and early 1970s, the bureau improved its price estimates and began publishing figures adjusted for inflation. This reflected new concerns about "stagflation" in the economy—high unemployment rates combined with high rates of inflation, a relatively unusual combination of economic phenomena. Two severe recessions occurred during this period, one from 1973–75 and the other from 1981–82 (during which the unemployment rate peaked at 10.8 percent, higher than it did during the Great Recession of 2007–2009). In both instances, the root cause was the shock of a sharp increase in oil prices. GDP figures declined significantly during both of these periods.

A shorter recession occurred in between the two severe ones. Levels of inflation skyrocketed, reaching 13.3 percent by 1979. The Federal Reserve reacted by sharply raising interest rates. This finally reined in inflation by removing money from the economy and leveling off rising prices. But the lack of cash circulating through the economy then worsened the severity of the ensuing economic downturn.

A brief recession also occurred during 1990–91, followed by an almost two-decade-long stretch of economic growth, interrupted by a mild recession from 2001–2002.

THE GREAT RECESSION OF 2007–2009

The scale of the Great Recession took most economists by surprise. The root cause of the economic downturn was a housing bubble. In the previous years, record numbers of people had taken out loans in order to buy their own homes. Many of these people could not actually afford to repay these loans. Defaults on mortgages began to rise, housing values sank, and the so-called housing bubble burst. The impact rippled throughout the entire economy. Big banks that had invested in mortgage debt had to be bailed out by the government, and stock market figures spiraled downward. Consumer spending fell, which affected corporate profits. With a lack of consumer demand, production declined, and businesses were forced to

The collapse of the housing market that heralded the Great Recession of 2007–2009 began with a record number of defaults on home loans. This led to foreclosures—when the bank that owns the loan seizes the home from the borrower. Many of these seized houses were then sold at rock-bottom prices at public auction.

lay off workers, further choking off consumer spending and generating a vicious downward economic spiral.

Economic growth declined significantly over the course of the Great Recession. The year 2008 saw a 0.0 percent level of

real GDP growth. Real GDP declined by 2.6 percent over the course of 2009. The steepest decline in quarterly GDP occurred at the end of 2008, when the rate of growth was -6.8 percent.

The Great Recession ended in 2009, and the economy began a gradual recovery. Many economic indicators, such as consumer spending, industrial production, and stock market figures, rebounded. The slump in the housing market persisted long after the official end of the recession. The Federal Reserve kept interest rates at unprecedented low levels to avoid hampering the recovery and to boost business and consumer spending. The unemployment rate peaked in late 2009 at a rate of 10.2 percent and then gradually began to fall. The U.S. economy was on the road to recovery.

GLOSSARY

business cycle Alternating periods of growth and contraction in the economy.

consumer A person or organization that purchases and uses economic goods, especially for personal, rather than commercial, use.

currency Something that is used as a medium of exchange; money.

demand The amount of a good or service that purchasers will buy at a given price.

depreciation A decrease in something's value due to deterioration, use, wear and tear, etc.

depression A prolonged economic downturn (or trough in the business cycle) marked by high unemployment levels.

fiscal policy The use of government spending and taxing powers to influence economic activity.

gross domestic product (GDP) The monetary value of all the goods and services produced in a nation during a period of time, usually a year.

gross national product (GNP) The monetary value of all goods and services produced by labor and property supplied by the residents of a country.

inflation An increase in general price levels of goods and services.

interest A sum paid or charged for the use of money or for borrowing money, often expressed as a percentage of money borrowed and to be paid back within a given time.

monetary policy Actions taken by a central bank (such as the Federal Reserve in the United States) to change the money supply in order to influence economic activity.

per capita GDP A measure of GDP divided by the number of people in a country.

profit The money left to a producer or employer after costs such as wages, rent, and raw materials are paid.

recession An economic downturn, usually defined as six months or more of declining GDP.

recovery The upward phase of the business cycle in which economic conditions improve.

FOR MORE INFORMATION

Bank of Canada
234 Wellington Street
Ottawa, ON K1A 0G9
Canada
(800) 303-1282
Web site: http://www.bankofcanada.ca
The Bank of Canada is the country's central bank.

Board of Governors of the Federal Reserve System
20th Street and Constitution Avenue NW
Washington, DC 20551
Web site: http://www.federalreserve.gov
The Federal Reserve is the central bank of the United States.

Bureau of Economic Analysis (BEA)
1441 L Street NW
Washington, DC 20230
(202) 606-9900
Web site: http://www.bea.gov
Part of the Department of Commerce, the BEA produces
    accounts statistics on the American economy.

International Monetary Fund (IMF)
700 19th Street NW

Washington, DC 20431
(202) 623-7000
Web site: http://www.imf.org
The IMF is an international economic organization made up
    of 187 nations.

National Economists Club
P.O. Box 19281
Washington, DC 20036
(703) 493-8824
Web site: http://www.national-economists.org
The National Economists Club is a nonprofit, nonpartisan
    organization with the goal of encouraging and sponsoring
    discussion and an exchange of ideas on economic trends
    and issues that are relevant to public policy.

Statistics Canada
150 Tunney's Pasture Driveway
Ottawa, ON K1A 0T6
Canada
(613) 951-8116
Web site: http://www.statcan.gc.ca
Statistics Canada is the government agency that produces
    statistics on its population, resources, economy, society,
    and culture.

U.S. Department of the Treasury
1500 Pennsylvania Avenue NW
Washington, DC 20220
(202) 622-2000
Web site: http://www.treas.gov

The Department of the Treasury's mission is to maintain a strong economy and create economic and job opportunities by promoting the conditions that enable economic growth and stability at home and abroad; strengthening national security by combating threats and protecting the integrity of the financial system; and managing the U.S. government's finances and resources effectively.

World Bank
1818 H Street NW
Washington, DC 20433
(202) 473-1000
Web site: http://www.worldbank.org
The World Bank provides financial and technical assistance to developing nations around the world.

WEB SITES

Due to the changing nature of Internet links, Rosen Publishing has developed an online list of Web sites related to the subject of this book. This site is updated regularly. Please use this link to access the list:

http://www.rosenlinks.com/rwe/gdp

FOR FURTHER READING

Acton, Johnny, and David Goldblatt. *Economy*. New York, NY: DK, 2010.

Antell, Gerson. *Economics for Everybody*. New York, NY: Amsco School Publications, 2006.

Clifford, Tim. *Our Economy in Action*. Vero Beach, FL: Rourke Publishing, LLC, 2009.

Craats, Rennay. *Economy: USA Past Present Future*. New York, NY: Weigl Publishers, 2009.

Gorman, Tom. *The Complete Idiot's Guide to the Great Recession*. New York, NY: Penguin Group, 2010.

Hall, Alvin. *Show Me the Money: How to Make Cents of Economics*. New York, NY: DK, 2008.

Landau, Elaine. *The Great Depression*. New York, NY: Children's Press, 2006.

Merino, Noel. *The World Economy* (Current Controversies). San Diego, CA: Greenhaven Press, 2010.

Miller, Debra A. *The U.S. Economy* (Current Controversies). San Diego, CA: Greenhaven Press, 2010.

Steger, Manfred. *Globalization: A Very Short Introduction*. New York, NY: Oxford University Press, 2009.

Teller-Elsberg, Jonathan, et al. *Field Guide to the U.S. Economy: A Compact and Irreverent Guide to Economic Life in America*. New York, NY: The New Press, 2006.

BIBLIOGRAPHY

Bureau of Economic Analysis. "Gross Domestic Product: Fourth Quarter and Annual 2010 (Third Estimate)." March 25, 2011. Retrieved March 2011 (http://www .bea.gov/newsreleases/national/gdp/2011/pdf/ gdp4q10_3rd.pdf).

Bureau of Economic Analysis. "Gross Domestic Product as a Measure of U.S. Production." August 1991. Retrieved March 2011 (http://www.bea.gov/scb/pdf/national/ nipa/1991/0891od.pdf).

Bureau of Economic Analysis. "Interactive Access to National Income and Product Accounts Tables." Retrieved March 2011 (http://www.bea.gov/national/ nipaweb/Index.asp).

Bureau of Economic Analysis. "Measuring the Economy: A Primer on GDP and the National Income and Product Accounts." September 2007. Retrieved March 2011 (http://www.bea.gov/national/pdf/nipa_ primer.pdf).

The Economist. Guide to Economic Indicators: Making Sense of Economics. 6th ed. New York, NY: Bloomberg Press, 2007.

Epping, Randy Charles. *The 21st Century Economy: A Beginner's Guide.* New York, NY: Vintage Books, 2009.

Flynn, Sean Masaki. *Economics for Dummies*. Hoboken, NJ: John Wiley & Sons, Inc., 2005.

Gertner, John. "The Rise and Fall of the G.D.P." *New York Times*, May 13, 2010. Retrieved March 2011 (http://www.nytimes.com/2010/05/16/magazine/16GDP-t.html?_r=1&scp=1&sq=rise%20and%20fall%20of%20the%20GDP&st=cse).

Graff, Amy. "Stay-at-Home Mom Salary: $117,856." SFGate, May 10, 2010. Retrieved March 2011 (http://www.sfgate.com/cgi-bin/blogs/sfmoms/detail?entry_id=63196#ixzz1FlSWrMlq).

International Monetary Fund. "World Economic and Financial Surveys: World Economic Outlook Database." 2010. Retrieved March 2011 (http://www.imf.org/external/pubs/ft/weo/2010/02/weodata/index.aspx).

Kuznets, Simon. "National Income, 1929–32." Senate Document No. 124, 73rd Congress, 2nd Session. Washington, DC: U.S. Government Printing Office, 1934.

Lanigan, Jane, ed. *Economics: Economic Theory*, Vol. 5. Danbury, CT: Grolier Educational, 2000.

Marcuss, Rosemary D., and Richard E. Kane. "U.S. National Income and Product Statistics: Born of the Great Depression and World War II." *Survey of Current Business*. Bureau of Economic Analysis, Vol. 87, No. 2, 2-2007.

Riggs, Thomas, ed. *Everyday Finance: Economics, Personal Money Management, and Entrepreneurship*. Detroit, MI: Gale Group, 2008.

Rowe, Jonathan. "Our Phony Economy." *Harper's*, June 2008. Retrieved March 2011 (http://www.harpers.org/archive/2008/06/0082042).

Samuelson, Paul A., and William D. Nordhaus. "GDP: One of the Great Inventions of the 20th Century." Bureau of Economic Analysis, January 2000. Retrieved March 2011 (http://www.bea.gov/scb/account_articles/general/0100od/maintext.htm).

Schneider, Friedrich, et al. "Shadow Economies All Over the World: New Estimates for 162 Countries from 1999 to 2007 (Revised Version)." Policy Research Working Paper Series. The World Bank, October 20, 2010. Retrieved March 2011 (http://www.econ.jku.at/members/Schneider/files/publications/LatestResearch2010/ShadEcWorld10_2010.pdf).

Tucker, Irvin. *Economics for Today*. 3rd ed. Mason, OH: Thomson Learning, 2003.

U.N. Development Programme. *Human Development Report 2010 – The Real Wealth of Nations: Pathways to Human Development*. New York, NY: Palgrave Macmillan, 2010.

Wheelan, Charles. *Naked Economics: Undressing the Dismal Science*. New York, NY: W. W. Norton and Company, 2002.

White House. *Economic Report of the President*. Washington, DC: U.S. Government Printing Office, 2011.

Wolverson, Roya. "GDP and Economic Policy." Council on Foreign Relations, September 10, 2010. Retrieved March 2011 (http://www.cfr.org/issue/economics/ri2v).

World Bank. "Indicators." Retrieved March 2011 (http://data. worldbank.org/indicator).

World Development Indicators Database. "Gross Domestic Product 2009, PPP." World Bank, December 15, 2010. Retrieved March 2011 (http://siteresources. worldbank.org/DATASTATISTICS/Resources/ GDP_PPP.pdf).

Yahoo! News. "China Could Overtake US Economy by 2030: WBank." March 23, 2011. Retrieved March 2011 (http://news.yahoo.com/s/afp/20110323/ts_alt_ afp/chinaeconomygrowthworldbank_ 20110323071834).

INDEX

About the Author

Corona Brezina is a writer who often writes on economic subjects. She has previously written books on stimulus plans, deflation, recession, imports and exports, commodities and futures trading, and the Federal Reserve and monetary policy. She lives in Chicago, Illinois.

Photo Credits

Cover (ship), pp. 1, 40–41, 52–53 Shutterstock; cover (headline) © www.istockphoto.com/Lilli Day; pp. 6–7, 24–25 © AP Images; pp. 4–5, 8, 20, 31, 43, 57 from photo by Mario Tama/Getty Images; p. 9 Yellow Dog Productions/Riser/Getty Images; pp. 10–11, 36–37 Bloomberg/Bloomberg via Getty Images; p. 13 © www.istockphoto.com/Matthew Hollinshead; pp. 16–17 Erik Dreyer/Taxi/Getty Images; p. 22 © www.istockphoto.com/philpell; pp. 29 Tim Boyle/Getty Images; p. 32 AFP/Getty Images; p. 34 John Foxx/Stockbyte/Thinkstock; pp. 44–45 D Dipasupil/ FilmMagic/Getty Images; pp. 46–47 Spencer Grant/ Getty Images; pp. 48–49 Mike Clarke/AFP/Getty Images; p. 55 © www.istockphoto.com/Ben Blankenburg; p. 58 Bureau of Economic Analysis; p. 59 AFP/Getty Images; pp. 60–61 Hulton Archive/Getty Images; pp. 62–63 Buyenlarge/Archive Photos/Getty Images; pp. 66–67 Justin Sullivan/Getty Images. Cover and interior graphic elements: © www.istockphoto.com/Andrey Prokhorov (front cover), © www.istockphoto.com/Dean Turner (back cover and interior pages), © www.istockphoto.com/Darja Tokranova (pp. 27, 28); © www.istockphoto.com/studiovision (pp. 68, 70, 73, 74, 78); © www.istockphoto.com/Chen Fu Soh (multiple interior pages).

Designer: Nicole Russo
Photo Researcher: Marty Levick